? COMMUNITY · CONNECTIONS

CELL PHONES FOR SOLDIERS
CHARITIES STARTED BY KIDS!
BY MELISSA SHERMAN PEARL AND DAVID A. SHERMAN

CHERRY LAKE
Publishing

Published in the United States of America by Cherry Lake Publishing
Ann Arbor, Michigan
www.cherrylakepublishing.com

Reading Adviser: Marla Conn MS, Ed., Literacy specialist, Read-Ability, Inc.

Photo Credits: Photos used with permission from Cell Phones for Soldiers, Cover, 1, 7, 9, 15, 17, 19, 21; © michaeljung / Shutterstock.com, 5; © Straight 8 Photography / Shutterstock.com, 11; © Jakub Krechowicz / Shutterstock.com, 13

LIBRARY OF CONGRESS CATALOGING-IN-PUBLICATION DATA HAS BEEN FILED AND IS AVAILABLE AT CATALOG.LOC.GOV

Cherry Lake Publishing would like to acknowledge the work of The Partnership for 21st Century Learning. Please visit *www.p21.org* for more information.

Printed in the United States of America
Corporate Graphics

CONTENTS

HOW DO THEY HELP?

COMMUNICATION NEEDS

Every year, between 150,000 and 200,000 United States military men and women are **deployed** throughout the world. These brave **troops** work hard day and night in foreign countries to protect our country's freedoms.

But soldiers may not have much access to phones, and when they do, calls are expensive.

Soldiers in the U.S. Armed Forces are mothers, fathers, daughters, sons, sisters, and brothers. They all have family back home waiting for them.

Think about what it would be like to be so far away from your friends and family. How do you think soldiers kept in touch with loved ones before cell phones? Do you communicate with people using a method other than a cell phone?

5

Cell Phones for Soldiers helps members of the U.S. Armed Forces keep in touch with the people they love. The organization has given more than 220 million minutes of free talk time to soldiers. It also helps **veterans** who have returned home.

Before we could use Internet-based applications to make phone calls, long distance cell phone bills could get very expensive.

MAKE A GUESS!

Are you able to guess how Cell Phones for Soldiers helps veterans who have already arrived home?

A CALL TO ACTION

In 2004, Brittany and Robbie Bergquist (then 13 and 12 years old) heard a local story that made them sad. An American soldier returned from Iraq with a nearly $8,000 cell phone bill. Thinking about their two cousins who were deployed, the **siblings** went from sad to mad. "Why would someone serving his country have to pay to talk to his family?" they wondered.

Soldiers have to travel where their orders take them. Sometimes that's very far from loved ones.

MAKE A GUESS!

Can you guess who is in charge of the United States military? If you said the president of the United States, you're right!

9

Robbie and Brittany decided to pay this soldier's bill. With $21 from their piggy banks, they went to the local bank to open an account and start saving. The bank manager was so impressed that he added $500 to their account.

While this was a good beginning, it wasn't enough. First they got donations. They held car washes and bake sales. The bank account grew. But it still wasn't enough to pay the soldier's bill.

Soldiers returning home are often faced with bills and medical expenses.

LOOK!

Look online or at the library to see what other charities help our armed forces. Find one that you may be interested in and learn more about it.

11

After a TV news program announced the name of their charity, Cell Phones for Soldiers, people started sending them old cell phones. They received around 15,000 devices. What would they do with all of them?

They couldn't simply add minutes to the phones and send them overseas. Not all phones worked in all countries. More importantly, the phone signal could possibly give away a soldier's

Cell Phones for Soldiers was started with just $21 from the siblings' piggy banks.

LOOK!

Does Cell Phones for Soldiers have collection locations in your area? Go to its Web site and see.

13

location. The U.S. military would not allow this.

Although the phones couldn't be used overseas, they could be recycled! And the two could even get money back for recycling them! The pair began sorting the cell phones for recycling. Using the earnings, the two bought prepaid phone cards for troops overseas.

Collecting cell phones was just the start of what Robbie and Brittany have been able to accomplish with their organization.

ASK QUESTIONS!

What other issues do you think soldiers have to deal with? Do you think it's different for men and women? Search online or at the library for answers to these and other questions.

THE FAMILY CELL PHONE PLAN

Robbie and Brittany have grown up alongside Cell Phones for Soldiers, and they work closely with two other Bergquists: their parents. Robert is a retired middle school science teacher who also serves as president and accountant of the organization. Gail is a retired special education teacher who handles communication.

Prepaid cell phone cards let soldiers make calls to loved ones without risking a big bill.

Have you or anyone you know ever donated a phone to Cell Phones for Soldiers? Ask your friends and family.

Across the country, small businesses, libraries, police stations, and fire stations volunteer their space for drop-off boxes. People can donate their old cell phones and tablets at more than 4,000 locations nationwide.

As technology has **evolved**, it has become easier to stay connected. These advances have allowed Cell Phones for Soldiers to use funds in other ways.

One of those other ways is to provide **grants** to help veterans ease

The Bergquist family is proud of the things Cell Phones for Soldiers has been able to provide for veterans.

CREATE!

Show what making a difference looks like. Put together a care package that you could send to a soldier. What things would you include, and why?

back into **civilian** life. Since July 2012, it has helped more than 2,800 veterans with **assimilation** hardships. They have delivered communication services, car repairs, and home payments.

Robbie, who is now Director, and Brittany continue to be involved with the organization. They are amazed that what started with $21 has surpassed $15 million. They have recycled 11.7 million cell phones and helped thousands of soldiers and veterans. Not bad for a couple of kids!

Robbie and Brittany were kids dedicated to helping those who had served the United States.

VIDE A LIFELINE
FOR
RICA'S BRAVEST
1. Power off device.
2. Drop device in the box.
PLEASE DONATE

STAR PLAZA ENTRY

EDS BENEFIT
DUTY TROOPS
VETERANS

LL PHONES
★ FOR ★
OLDIERS

LINE
VEST

cling proudly supports and
ly recycles on behalf of

nesforsoldiers.com

PROCEEDS BENEFIT
ACTIVE-DUTY TROOPS
AND VETERANS

CELL PHONES
★ FOR ★
SOLDIERS

★

Dynamic Recycling proudly supports and
responsibly recycles on behalf of
cellphonesforsoldiers.com

STAPLE
Cente
green tea

THINK!

What are the five
main branches of the
military, and what
are the differences
between them?

GLOSSARY

assimilation (uh-sim-uh-LAY-shuhn) the process of adapting or adjusting to the culture of a group or nation

civilian (suh-VIL-yuhn) a person who is not a member of the armed forces or a police or firefighting force

deployed (dih-PLOID) moved out for a specific purpose

evolved (ih-VAHLVD) developed gradually

grants (GRANTS) amounts of money donated by the government or an organization for a specific purpose and that needn't be repaid

siblings (SIB-lingz) brothers or sisters

troops (TROOPS) groups of soldiers

veterans (VET-ur-uhnz) people who have served in a military force, especially those who have fought in a war

FIND OUT MORE

WEB SITES

www.cellphonesforsoldiers.com
Learn more about the Bergquist family and what they do.

www.oidelivers.org
Operation Interdependence is a nonprofit organization that provides a means for community members to support troops serving on the front lines, military families, and veterans.

www.sesamestreetformilitaryfamilies.org
A gentle source of information specifically for military families.

INDEX

ABOUT THE AUTHORS

David Sherman and Melissa Sherman Pearl are cousins who understand and appreciate that you don't have to be an adult to make a difference.